Modern American English

Robert J. Dixson

As Revised by Eugene J. Hall

Workbook

3

New Edition

REGENTS/PRENTICE HALL, Englewood Cliffs, New Jersey 07632

Publisher: Tina B. Carver
Manager of Product Development: Mary Vaughn
Senior Development Editor: Nancy L. Leonhardt
Senior Production Editor: Tunde A. Dewey
Interior design and page layout: Function Through Form
Design supervision: Chris Wolf
Prepress buyer: Ray Keating
Manufacturing buyer: Lori Bulwin

Cover design: Bruce Kenselaar
Cover photograph:© John Kelly/The Image Bank

Printed in the United States of America

10 9 8 7 6 5 4 3 2

ISBN 0-13-594045-1

Prentice-Hall International (UK) Limited, *London*
Prentice-Hall of Australia Pty. Limited, *Sydney*
Prentice-Hall Canada Inc., *Toronto*
Prentice-Hall Hispanoamericana, S.A., *Mexico*
Prentice-Hall of India Private Limited, *New Delhi*
Prentice-Hall of Japan, Inc., *Tokyo*
Simon & Schuster Asia Pte. Ltd., *Singapore*
Editora Prentice-Hall do Brasil, Ltda., *Rio de Janeiro*

Contents

Foreword

This workbook provides additional practice in comprehension, speaking, reading, and writing for students using *Modern American English 3*. The lessons in the workbook are closely coordinated with those in the book; there are fifteen lessons in the workbook as in the book, and every fifth lesson is a review of material that has been previously introduced. Each workbook lesson should be assigned after the corresponding lesson in the book has been covered in class.

The lessons are divided into three sections: Vocabulary Study; Structure and Pattern Practice; and Reading and Conversation Practice. The Vocabulary Study section is omitted from the three review lessons. Each section strengthens the development of all the language skills.

The first part of the Vocabulary Study includes a number of sentences that contain examples of the structural patterns that are covered in the lesson. Some vocabulary items beyond those given in the book are also given in these sentences. They are cued to pictures, and the students give answers to questions cued to the same or similar pictures. The teacher first goes over the sentences by means of choral and individual repetition, followed by individual students reading aloud. The second part of the Vocabulary Study is the question and answer practice. First the teacher prepares the students by means of choral and individual repetition of both questions and answers. Then individual students give the answers when the teacher asks the questions. If time permits, student-student practice, with one student asking the questions and another giving the answers, is valuable. Spaces are left so that the students can write their answers in the workbook itself.

The third part of the Vocabulary Study introduces additional vocabulary—idiomatic phrases, for example, or irregular verbs. This additional vocabulary appears at some point in the lesson. These sentences are intended for presentation by choral and individual repetition and reading aloud by individual students.

The second section, Structure and Pattern Practice, corresponds to the same section in the book lessons. Additional exercises are given on the grammatical material covered in the book. The same procedures are suggested—choral and individual repetition of both cues and responses, followed by individual responses as the teacher gives the cues. Again, if time permits, student-student practice will be helpful. The exercises are principally of three types: (1) those in which the students complete a sentence by filling in the correct form; (2) those in which the students make a change from one pattern to another; and (3) those in which the students combine two sentences into one. The workbook provides spaces in which the students can write their responses to the cues in these exercises. One of the principal uses of this section is for written homework.

The third section, Reading and Conversation Practice, includes a short reading and a dialogue. As more structures are introduced, a more natural mixture of structures is presented in both the reading and the dialogue, although there is an emphasis on the structural material that is presented in that particular lesson. The reading is followed by comprehension questions. Again, there are spaces in which the students can write the answers to these questions. The usual procedures for reading and question and answer practice should be followed for the reading and comprehension sections.

The dialogue is also presented in the same manner, but are followed by student-student practice if this is possible. In addition, the students can memorize the dialogue or write new ones of a similar nature as a homework assignment. The students can then act out the dialogues in class as short plays.

The study of the structure and grammatical forms of a language does not always provide students with sufficient experience to understand or participate in a conversation in the language which they are trying to learn, or even to get as much out of reading as they would like. These workbooks give additional practice beyond that in the books so that students can develop the skills necessary for effective understanding and use of the language, whether that may involve reading, writing, or conversation. In short, when used with the books, these workbooks give students the broadest possible classroom experience.

LESSON

1

ONE

Vocabulary Study

A. Study.

1. There was a lot of excitement in the cafeteria yesterday evening.

2. There was a fire in the kitchen.

3. The cafeteria filled up with smoke.

4. All the students ran outside.

5. A fire truck arrived in a few minutes.

6. It only took about a quarter of an hour to put out the fire.

7. Luckily there wasn't much damage.

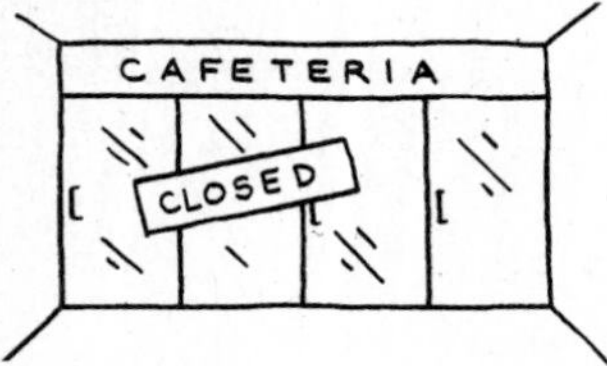

8. The cafeteria is closed today.

9. It will open again tomorrow.

> *Ran* is the past tense of the irregular verb *to run.*
>
> She runs to class every morning.
> I ran to the store to get some aspirin.

B. Answer the questions.

1. When was there a lot of excitement in the cafeteria?

1. ______________________

____

2. Why was there a lot of excitement?

2. ______________________

____

3. What happened in the cafeteria?

3. ______________________

____

4. What did the students do?

4. ______________________

5. When did a fire truck arrive?

5. ______________________
____

6. How long did it take to put out the fire?

6. ______________________
____

7. Was there a lot of damage?

7. ______________________
____

8. Is the cafeteria open today?

8. ______________________
____

9. When will it be open again?

9. ______________________
____

C. Study.

1. Isn't the cafeteria open today?
No, it isn't.

2. Aren't there always a lot of students in the cafeteria?
Yes, there are.

3. It wasn't a very big fire, was it?
No, it wasn't.

4. There wasn't much damage, was there?
   No, there wasn't.

5. They were lucky, weren't they?
   Yes, they were.

Structure and Pattern Practice

A. Change to the present tense.

EXAMPLE

It was very cold. — *It's very cold.*

1. There was a committee to decorate the gym. 1. ______
2. His desk was untidy. 2. ______
3. They were at the supermarket. 3. ______
4. She was in the kitchen. 4. ______
5. I was downstairs. 5. ______

B. Change to the past tense.

EXAMPLE

The letter is on my desk. — *The letter was on my desk.*

1. Anita and Pete are in the gym. 1. ______
2. The factory is closed. 2. ______
3. I'm very hungry. 3. ______
4. The lecture is very important. 4. ______
5. There's a message on your desk. 5. ______

C. Change to the negative.

EXAMPLE

She's at her desk now. — *She isn't at her desk now.*

1. I was late this morning. 1. ______________________
2. He's a farmer. 2. ______________________
3. The knives and forks are on the table. 3. ______________________
____
4. She's on vacation this week. 4. ______________________
5. We were very thirsty. 5. ______________________

D. Change first to an affirmative question and then to a negative question.

EXAMPLE

She's at her desk now. — *Is she at her desk now?*

Isn't she at her desk now?

1. There's a bank around the corner. 1. ______________________
____
2. He's a good carpenter. 2. ______________________
____
3. Her books are in the car. 3. ______________________
____
4. The cafeteria was closed yesterday. 4. ______________________
____
5. The dishes were on the top shelf. 5. ______________________
____
6. We were very busy yesterday. (you) 6. ______________________
____

7. She's in a special English class. 7. ______________________________

____

8. I'm an engineering student. (you) 8. ______________________________

____

E. Complete with the appropriate attached questions.

EXAMPLE

It's a beautiful day, *isn't it?*

1. The dance was a lot of fun, ____________?
2. These packages are heavy, ____________?
3. The exam wasn't very difficult, ____________?
4. You aren't sick, ____________?
5. She's very lucky, ____________?
6. There's some chalk in the box, ____________?
7. There was a field trip last week, ____________?
8. There weren't any holidays last month, ____________?

Reading and Conversation Practice

A. Read.

Fire is always a danger. There was a big fire at Washington College in 1985. The administration building burned down. The fire destroyed many of the student records.

Now the college has its own fire department. There are two fire trucks and an ambulance in a building on campus. There are always firefighters on duty.

Last month there was a fire in the dormitory. It started in a wastebasket. The firefighters put that fire out in a couple of minutes. Then last night there was a fire in the cafeteria kitchen. The fire truck arrived in five minutes. There was a lot of smoke but not much fire. It was out after fifteen minutes. The students cheered the firefighters.

> *Its* is the possessive adjective form for *it*. *Own* is used after possessive forms to make them more emphatic.

B. Answer these questions.

1. What is always a danger? 1. ____________________
2. When was there a big fire at Washington College? 2. ____________________
3. What burned down? 3. ____________________
4. What did the fire destroy? 4. ____________________
5. What does the college have now? 5. ____________________
6. What is there in a building on campus? 6. ____________________
7. Who is always on duty? 7. ____________________
8. Where was there a fire last month? 8. ____________________
9. Where did it start? 9. ____________________
10. How long did it take for the firefighters to put it out? 10. ____________________
11. Where was there a fire last night? 11. ____________________
12. When did the fire truck arrive? 12. ____________________
13. Was it a big fire? 13. ____________________
14. When was the fire out? 14. ____________________
15. What did the students do? 15. ____________________

C. Dialogue

DEBBIE: I'm hungry.
BOB: Yes, I'm hungry too.
DEBBIE: And I'm thirsty.
BOB: But the cafeteria is closed today.
DEBBIE: That fire was really exciting, wasn't it?
BOB: Yes, it was. There was a lot of smoke.
DEBBIE: But it didn't do much damage.
BOB: Those firefighters are really great, aren't they?
DEBBIE: Yes, they are. They got there in just a couple of minutes.
BOB: And then it only took them a couple more to put out the fire.
DEBBIE: Yes, they were fast. But I'm still hungry. And thirsty too.
BOB: There's a hamburger place in town.
DEBBIE: Yes, but it's a long way from the campus, isn't it?
BOB: Oh, it isn't too far.
DEBBIE: Can I get a milkshake there too?
BOB: Oh, sure. Come on, we can walk there in a few minutes.

Additional Vocabulary

administration
always
ambulance
(to) burn (down)
(to) cheer
damage (n)
danger
(to) destroy
(on) duty

excitement
exciting
(to) fill (up with)
fire (n)
firefighter
its
luckily
lucky

more
outside
own
(to) put out
record (n)
(to) run
smoke (n)
sure

Vocabulary Study

A. Study.

1. Steve West works in sales.

2. He always has a lot of figures to check.

3. He uses a computer at work.

4. Last month he bought a computer to use at home.

5. He taught his wife Laura how to use it.

6. Now Steve brings a lot of work home.

7. They use the computer to plan their budget.

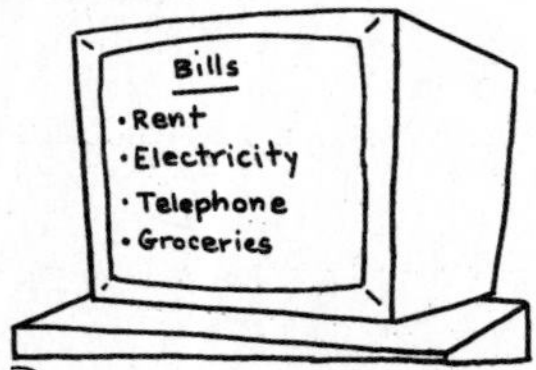

8. They also use it to pay their bills.

9. Laura uses it to plan meals.

> *To pay* is also an irregular verb. The past tense form is *paid*.
>
> They always pay their bills on the first of the month.
> He paid a lot for the computer.

B. Answer the questions.

1. What does Steve West do?

1. ____________________

2. What does he always have to do?

2. ____________________
____

3. What does he use at work?

3. ____________________

4. What did he buy last month?

4. ____________________

5. Who is Laura? What did Steve teach her?

5. ______________________

____

6. What does Steve bring home now?

6. ______________________

____

7. What do they use the computer for?

7. ______________________

____

8. What else do they use it for?

8. ______________________

____

9. What does Laura use it for?

9. ______________________

____

C. Study.

1. Doesn't she know how to use a computer?
No, she doesn't.

2. Don't they use the computer to pay their bills?
Yes, they do.

3. Didn't he teach her how to use the computer?
Yes, he did.

4. She learned how to use the computer, didn't she?
   Yes, she did.

5. He always brings home a lot of work, doesn't he?
   Yes, he does.

6. They don't work in the city, do they?
   No, they don't.

Structure and Pattern Practice

A. Change to the present tense. Change *yesterday* to *every day.*

EXAMPLE

I worked late yesterday. *I work late every day.*

1. He brought some work home yesterday. 1. ____________________

2. She got up at six o'clock yesterday. 2. ____________________

3. They took the subway to work yesterday. 3. ____________________

4. I met her after work yesterday. 4. ____________________

B. Change to the past tense. Change *every day* to *yesterday.*

EXAMPLE

We go to school every day. *We went to school yesterday.*

1. She uses the computer every day. 1. ____________________

2. He drives to work every day. 2. ____________________

3. They watch television every day. 3. ____________________

4. I eat in the cafeteria every day. 4. ____________________

C. Change to the negative.

EXAMPLE

She walked to work. *She didn't walk to work.*

1. We began a new lesson yesterday. 1. ____________________

2. I sleep late every Saturday. 2. ____________________

3. They go shopping in the evening. 3. ____________________

____

4. We saw a movie last night. 4. ____________________

5. I know how to use a computer. 5. ____________________

6. She lives in the city. 6. ____________________

7. He washes his car every week. 7. ____________________

D. Change first to affirmative questions and then to negative questions.

EXAMPLE

She walked to work. *Did she walk to work?*

Didn't she walk to work?

1. He bought a computer. 1. ____________________

____

2. She files all the correspondence. 2. ____________________

____

3. The fire destroyed most of the student records. 3. ____________________

____

4. They ran outside. 4. ____________________

____

5. She leaves the office at five o'clock. 5. ______________________________

____

6. We use the computer every day. (you) 6. ______________________________

____

7. They enjoy the movies. 7. ______________________________

E. Complete with the appropriate attached questions.

EXAMPLE

She didn't drive to work yesterday, ___*did she?*___

1. He always brings a lot of work home, ______________?
2. You didn't finish your homework, ______________?
3. They went on a field trip last week, ______________?
4. He eats a lot of hamburgers, ______________?
5. She doesn't understand the lesson, ______________?
6. They don't work on Saturday, ______________?
7. They stayed at a hotel, ______________?
8. They read a lot of books, ______________?

Reading and Conversation Practice

A. Read.

Many people use personal computers nowadays. Several of the students at Washington College have computers in their rooms. Akira learned how to use a computer in Japan. He's an engineering student, so he has to work with a lot of figures. He bought a computer during his first week at Washington College. He uses it every day.

Bob doesn't have a computer. He doesn't have enough money to buy one. He uses Akira's computer when he has a lot of homework. Now he wants to save some money to buy his own computer. Ben doesn't have a computer either. He doesn't need one, he says. He studies history and English. He only takes one math course. Last month he tried to do his math homework on Akira's computer. He didn't finish it because he didn't understand how to use the computer.

B. Answer these questions.

1. What do many people use nowadays? 1. ______________________
2. What do several of the students at Washington College have? 2. ______________________
3. Where did Akira learn to use a computer? 3. ______________________
4. Why does he have to work with a lot of figures? 4. ______________________
5. When did he buy a computer? 5. ______________________
6. Does he use it much? 6. ______________________
7. Why doesn't Bob have a computer? 7. ______________________
8. When does he use Akira's computer? 8. ______________________
9. Why does he want to save some money now? 9. ______________________
10. Why doesn't Ben have a computer? 10. ______________________
11. What does he study? 11. ______________________
12. How many math courses does he take? 12. ______________________

13. What did he try to do last month? 13. ______________________

____

14. Why didn't he finish it? 14. ______________________

C. Dialogue

BEN: Did you hand in your history term paper?

ANITA: Yes, I did. I gave it to Professor Gomez yesterday.What about you?

BEN: I didn't finish my paper.

ANITA: Didn't finish it! Why not?

BEN: I want to change a few things.

ANITA: You did write a paper, didn't you?

BEN: Yes, but I want to improve it.

ANITA: You need a word processor.

BEN: Oh, I tried to use Akira's computer, but I didn't understand it.

ANITA: It's easy to make changes on a word processor.

BEN: Like what?

ANITA: You can move paragraphs around. You just need to press a key or two.

BEN: I don't know. I'm no good with mechanical things.

ANITA: Really, it's easy. You can put in a word or a sentence, and you don't have to type everything again.

BEN: Well, maybe I should think about it.

ANITA: Come on, I'll show you my word processor.

Additional Vocabulary

bill
budget
change (n)
figure (number)
(to) improve
mechanical
nowadays
paragraph
(to) pay
personal
(to) press
processor (word processor)
(to) put in
term paper

LESSON
3
THREE

Vocabulary Study

A. Study.

1. Anita is standing in front of the library.

2. She's waiting for Dan.

3. He promised to meet her at six o'clock.

4. She's looking at her watch. It's twenty after six.

5. It's getting dark.

6. It's also getting cold, and Anita isn't wearing a coat.

7. She's getting angry.

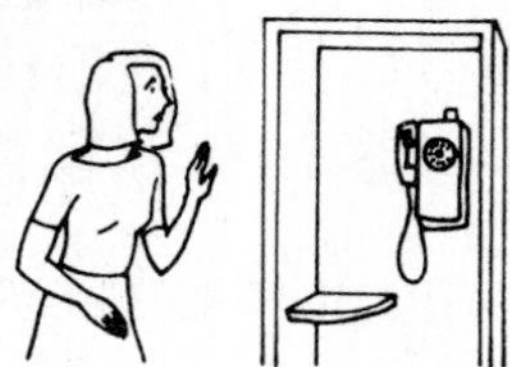

8. In a minute she's going inside the library to find a phone.

9. She's going to call Dan and tell him to forget their date.

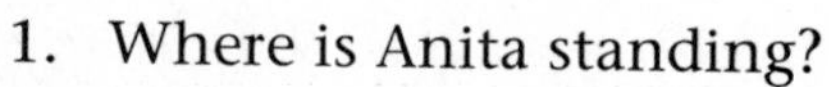

B. Answer the questions.

1. Where is Anita standing?

1. ____________________

2. Who's she waiting for?

2. ____________________

3. What did he promise?

3. ____________________

4. What's she looking at? What time is it?

4. ____________________

____

5. Is it getting dark?

5. ____________________

6. Is it getting cold too?
   Isn't Anita wearing a coat?

6. ______________________________
____

7. Is she getting angry?

7. ______________________________

8. What's she going to do in a minute?

8. ______________________________
____

9. Who's she going to call?
   What's she going to tell him?

9. ______________________________
____

C. Study.

1. He was sleeping when she called him.

2. We were walking across the campus when it began to snow.

3. They were sitting around the cafeteria when the fire started.

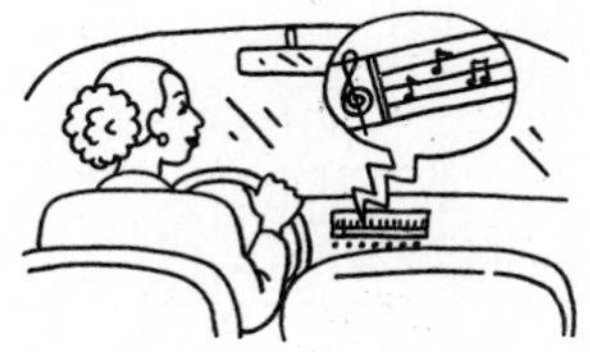

4. I was listening to the radio while I was driving to work.

5. She was playing the piano while I was cooking dinner.

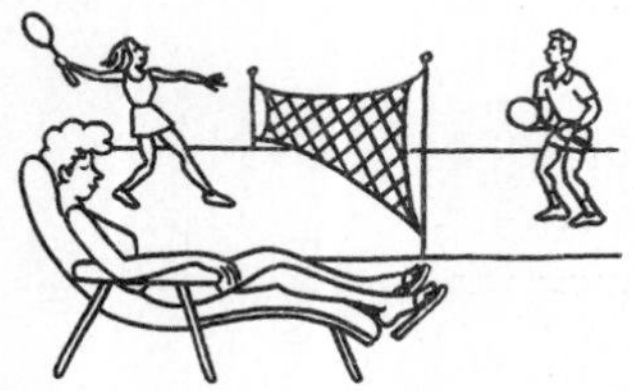

6. She was resting while her friends were playing tennis.

Structure and Pattern Practice

A. Change first to affirmative questions and then to negative questions.

EXAMPLE

She's wearing a coat. — *Is she wearing a coat?*

Isn't she wearing a coat?

1. I'm going to wait a few more minutes. (you) — 1. ______________________ ______________________
2. It was getting cold. — 2. ______________________ ______________________
3. They're going to build some houses here. — 3. ______________________ ______________________
4. We were playing basketball. (you) — 4. ______________________ ______________________
5. They're cleaning up the gym this morning. — 5. ______________________ ______________________
6. She's going to look for a new job. — 6. ______________________ ______________________
7. He's studying science. — 7. ______________________ ______________________

B. Complete with the appropriate attached questions.

EXAMPLE

They're planning a picnic, *aren't they?*

1. They're going to visit their parents, ____________________?
2. You weren't lying down, ____________________?
3. She was teaching chemistry last year, ____________________?
4. It isn't going to rain today, ____________________?
5. They're going on a field trip next week, ____________________?
6. He's going to see the doctor today, ____________________?
7. They aren't starting a new lesson today, ____________________?
8. She isn't teaching this year, ____________________?

C. Change the first sentence to the past continuous and then use *when* to connect them.

EXAMPLE

I drove to school. I saw her on the corner. — *I was driving to school when I saw her on the corner.*

1. It got dark. I finally went home. — 1. ____________________
2. He showed me his pictures. You came in. — 2. ____________________
3. She studied math. The phone rang. — 3. ____________________
4. I walked to school. It began to get very cold. — 4. ____________________
5. I ate a hamburger. The fire started. — 5. ____________________

D. Change both sentences to the past continuous and then use *while* to connect them.

EXAMPLE

It rained. We drove to work. *It was raining while we were driving to work.*

1. We listened to the radio. He slept. 1. ____________________

2. She read. She ate a sandwich. 2. ____________________

3. He read a book. He sat under the tree. 3. ____________________

4. My sister talked on the phone. We ate dinner. 4. ____________________

5. I filed the old correspondence. She took dictation. 5. ____________________

Reading and Conversation Practice

A. Read.

It's raining and it's cold this morning. Bob is walking across the campus. He isn't going to class this morning. He's going to see the college doctor. There's an infirmary in the administration building. The doctor there takes care of the students' health problems.

When Bob got to the infirmary, three other students were waiting to see the doctor. Bob sat down and looked at a magazine. He waited half an hour before the doctor called him. She took Bob's temperature. He had a fever. He also had a bad headache. The doctor gave him some aspirin. Then she told him to go back to his room and stay in bed.

B. Answer these questions.

1. How's the weather this morning? 1. ______________________________

____

2. What is Bob doing? 2. ______________________________

____

3. Is he going to class this morning? 3. ______________________________

____

4. What's he going to do? 4. ______________________________

5. Where is there an infirmary? 5. ______________________________

____

6. What does the doctor there do? 6. ______________________________

____

7. How many students were waiting to see the doctor? 7. ______________________________

____

8. What did Bob do? 8. ______________________________

____

9. How long did he wait before the doctor called him? 9. ______________________________

____

10. What did the doctor do? 10. ______________________________

____

11. What did Bob have? 11. ______________________________

12. What else did he have? 12. ______________________________

____

13. What did the doctor give him? 13. ______________________________

____

14. What did she tell him to do? 14. ______________________________

____

C. Dialogue

BOB: What were you doing last night?
DEBBIE: What time last night?
BOB: Between eight and nine o'clock.
DEBBIE: I was watching television.
BOB: Were you alone?
DEBBIE: My brother and I were watching TV together.
BOB: You weren't talking on the phone, were you?
DEBBIE: Me? No, I wasn't.
BOB: Who was then?
DEBBIE: Oh, my sister probably.
BOB: She was certainly talking for a long time.
DEBBIE: Yes, she does spend a lot of time on the phone. Why were you trying to get me?
BOB: I needed some help with a math problem.
DEBBIE: I'm sorry. Maybe I can help you next time.

Additional Vocabulary

between
(to) build [built]
dark
fever
headache
health
help (n)
infirmary
inside
(to) promise
temperature

LESSON

4

FOUR

Vocabulary Study

A. Study.

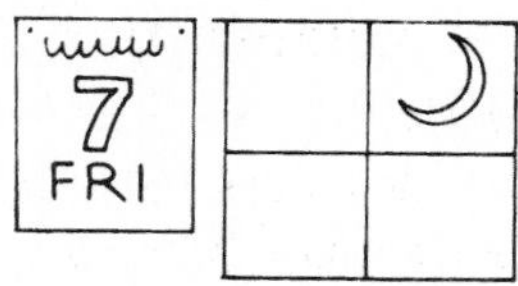

1. It's Friday evening.

2. Bob is tired. He just came home from work.

3. Ben wants him to go to a dance.

4. Bob has to work again tomorrow morning.

5. He has to be at the supermarket at seven o'clock.

6. He has to sweep the floor before the store opens.

7. He can't go to the dance.

8. He should go to bed early.

9. Then he'll be able to get up early and get to work on time.

B. Answer the questions.

1. Is it Friday or Saturday evening?

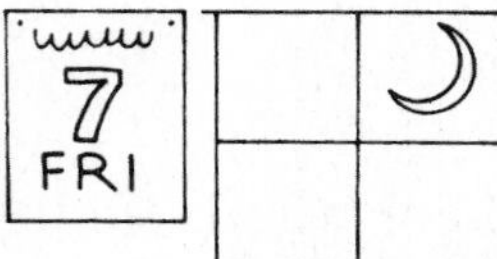

1. ______________________________
____

2. Why is Bob tired?

2. ______________________________

3. What does Ben want?

3. ______________________________

4. When does Bob have to work again?

4. ______________________________
____

5. When does he have to be at the supermarket?

5. ______________________________
____

6. When does he have to sweep the floor?

6. ______________________

____

7. Can he go to the dance?

7. ______________________

8. What should he do?

8. ______________________

9. What will he be able to do then?

9. ______________________

____

C. Study.

1. Bob got to his nine o'clock class at eight forty-five. He was early.

2. Dan got to his nine o'clock class at nine ten. He was late.

3. Ben got to his nine o'clock class at nine exactly. He was on time.

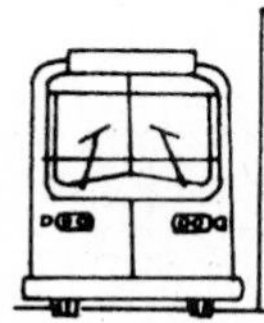

4. The four o'clock bus arrived at three fifty-five. It was early.

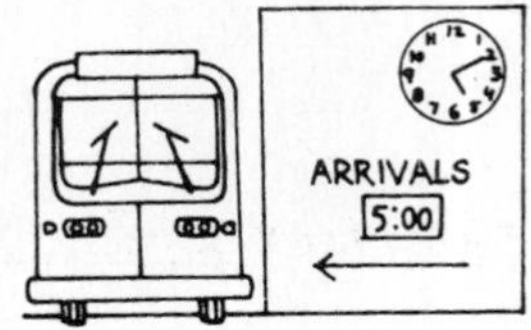

5. The five o'clock bus arrived at five ten. It was late.

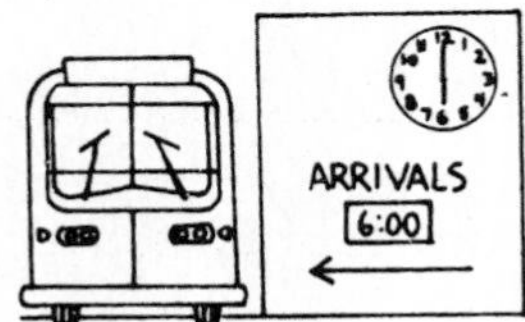

6. The six o'clock bus arrived at six exactly.
It was on time.

Structure and Pattern Practice

A. Answer these questions in complete sentences, using the phrase in parentheses.

EXAMPLE

How many of the questions can you answer? (I) (all the questions) — *I can answer all the questions.*

1. What time should he meet her? (at five o'clock) 1. ______
2. What must she finish tonight? (her term paper) 2. ______
3. When may I see my professor? (you) (tomorrow afternoon) 3. ______
4. When will we have another field trip? (next month) 4. ______
5. Where can I keep my bicycle? (you) (in the garage) 5. ______
6. Why must she go home early? (because she has an early class) 6. ______
7. Who should attend the meeting? (all the students) 7. ______

B. Change first to affirmative questions and then to negative questions.

EXAMPLE

She'll wait a few more minutes. *Will she wait a few more minutes?*

Won't she wait a few more minutes?

1. She can find a phone in the library. 1. ______________________

____

2. They'll have a holiday tomorrow. 2. ______________________

____

3. You can park on the street. (I) 3. ______________________

____

4. He'll work this summer. 4. ______________________

____

5. She should visit her parents. 5. ______________________

____

6. You should learn a foreign language. (we) 6. ______________________

____

C. Complete with the appropriate attached questions.

EXAMPLE

She should explain the lesson, *shouldn't she?*

1. He can improve his term paper, ______________________?
2. They won't have another field trip this month, ______________________?
3. He should try to be on time, ______________________?
4. She can't stay in bed today, ______________________?
5. She'll make some sandwiches for us, ______________________?
6. He shouldn't go to class today, ______________________?

D. Change *must* to *have to.*

EXAMPLE

I must get up early tomorrow. *I have to get up early tomorrow.*

1. He must sweep the floor. 1. ______
2. She must have another sandwich. 2. ______
3. We must be ready to leave at noon. 3. ______
4. He must find a part-time job. 4. ______
5. They must pay their tuition today. 5. ______

E. Change *should* to *ought to.*

EXAMPLE

They should study for the exam. *They ought to study for the exam.*

1. He shouldn't work all the time. 1. ______
2. They should give us more field trips. 2. ______
3. I should go to the bank today. 3. ______
4. They shouldn't stay out in the rain. 4. ______

F. Change *can* to *will be able to.*

EXAMPLE

I can finish my paper this weekend. *I'll be able to finish my paper this weekend.*

1. She can make some sandwiches for the picnic. 1. ______
2. I can meet you at three o'clock. 2. ______
3. You can find those words in the dictionary. 3. ______
4. She can't wait for him after noon. 4. ______

Reading and Conversation Practice

A. Read.

Ben is majoring in English and history, but he also has to take a science course every year. This year he has chemistry. There are three lecture hours and two lab hours every week.

He and Bob are reading their chemistry books now. They have to prepare for their lab hour tomorrow. They're getting ready to do an experiment. They'll have to be very careful. The experiment is a very difficult one. "You ought to know every step in the experiment before you come to class," the professor told them. "You can't be careless," she warned. "A mistake can cause an accident."

Ben and Bob are going over every step in the experiment. They ask each other questions about the experiment. Bob has to correct Ben when he gives the wrong answer. "I'll be able to do the experiment without a mistake," Ben finally tells Bob. Bob replies, "That's fine, but we ought to go over it again one more time."

B. Answer these questions.

1. What is Ben majoring in?	1. ____________________
2. What does he also have to take?	2. ____________________
3. What does he have this year?	3. ____________________
4. How many lecture and lab hours are there every week?	4. ____________________ ____________________
5. What are Ben and Bob doing now?	5. ____________________
6. What are they getting ready to do?	6. ____________________
7. Why will they have to be very careful?	7. ____________________ ____________________
8. What did the professor tell them?	8. ____________________
9. What are Ben and Bob going over?	9. ____________________ ____________________

10. What do they ask each other? 10. ______________________

11. When does Bob have to correct Ben? 11. ______________________

____

12. What does Ben finally tell Bob? 12. ______________________

13. What does Bob reply? 13. ______________________

C. Dialogue

Ben is talking to Professor Duval, his chemistry teacher.

BEN: This experiment—is it our final one for the year?

DR. DUVAL: Yes, it is.

BEN: When are we going to do it?

DR. DUVAL: We'll do it in the lab on Thursday.

BEN: Will we be able to finish it in one day?

DR. DUVAL: Yes, we'll have to.

BEN: Is it difficult?

DR. DUVAL: It isn't difficult, but you'll have to be very careful.

BEN: Why? Is it dangerous?

DR. DUVAL: Well, a mistake can cause an accident.

BEN: What do I need to do to prepare for the experiment?

DR. DUVAL: You ought to go over every step before you come to class.

BEN: I hope I understand it.

DR. DUVAL: You have to study, that's all.

Additional Vocabulary

accident
answer (n)
careless
(to) cause
(to) correct
dangerous
exactly
experiment (n)
(to) go over
lab (laboratory)
(to) major (in)
mistake
(to) prepare
step (n)
(to) warn
without

LESSON 5 FIVE

REVIEW

Structure and Pattern Practice

A. Change first to affirmative questions and then to negative questions.

EXAMPLE

It's a difficult experiment. — *Is it a difficult experiment?*

Isn't it a difficult experiment?

1. A mistake will cause an accident. 1. ______________________

____

2. She's majoring in chemistry. 2. ______________________

____

3. He was sick yesterday. 3. ______________________

____

4. She taught history last year. 4. ______________________

____

5. They should be very careful. 5. ______________________

____

6. He has to take a science course. 6. ______________________

____

7. They wash the car every week. 7. ______________________

____

8. We're going to have a dance next week. (you) 8. ______________________

____

B. Complete with the appropriate attached questions.

EXAMPLE

The experiment isn't dangerous, *is it?*

1. She made some sandwiches for the picnic, ________________?
2. There wasn't much damage, ________________?
3. He doesn't understand the experiment, ________________?
4. You'll be very careful, ________________?
5. We aren't going to have an exam next week, ________________?
6. I should go over every step in the experiment, ________________?
7. There isn't any place to park near the cafeteria, ________________?
8. You have two lab hours a week, ________________?

C. Change the first sentence to the past continuous. Then use *when* to combine it with the second sentence.

EXAMPLE

I drove to school. I saw her on the corner. — *I was driving to school when I saw her on the corner.*

1. He fixed his bicycle. We left. — 1. ________________
2. I paid my tuition. I saw my friends. — 2. ________________
3. They danced. We came in the gym. — 3. ________________
4. She wrote a letter. I arrived. — 4. ________________

D. Change both sentences to the past continuous and then use *while* to connect them.

EXAMPLE

She ate. I talked to her. — *She was eating while I was talking to her.*

1. I read the newspaper. He cooked dinner. — 1. ________________

2. Ben got gasoline. Bob washed the windshield. 2. ______________________

____

3. They talked. I studied. 3. ______________________

4. We had a picnic. They attended a lecture. 4. ______________________

____

E. Change *must* to *have to.*

EXAMPLE

You must be very careful. *You have to be very careful.*

1. You must get some gas. 1. ______________________

2. You must go over the experiment step by step. 2. ______________________

____

3. She must improve her term paper. 3. ______________________

4. I must learn how to use a word processor. 4. ______________________

____

5. He must meet her at five o'clock. 5. ______________________

F. Change *should* to *ought to.*

EXAMPLE

I should go to the library today. *I ought to go to the library today.*

1. You shouldn't be careless in the lab. 1. ______________________

2. You should check the oil too. 2. ______________________

3. I should help him with those math problems. 3. ______________________

____

4. She shouldn't drink a lot of coffee. 4. ______________________

5. We should go to the airport with him. 5. ______________________

G. Change *can* to *will be able to.*

EXAMPLE

They can't finish the experiment. — *They won't be able to finish the experiment.*

1. They can't fix my car this week. 1. ______
2. She can't go to the dance with me. 2. ______
3. He can't drive me to the airport. 3. ______
4. I can't go to the post office. 4. ______
5. They can't take another field trip. 5. ______

Reading and Conversation Practice

A. Read.

Ben needed some books for one of his English courses. He went to the college bookstore to find them. The students can buy all the books for their courses there. The store is in the basement of the administration building. Ben spends a lot of time there because he likes books. He reads two or three every week. He hopes that he'll be able to get a part-time job in the bookstore next year.

He was looking for a book when Anita came in. She asked Ben to help her pick out a book in English. Her English teacher told her she ought to read more. Ben showed her some paperbacks. Anita looked at them, but they weren't easy enough. Ben finally bought four books, but Anita didn't buy any.

B. Answer these questions.

1. What did Ben need? 1. ______
2. What can the students buy at the college bookstore? 2. ______
3. Where is the store? 3. ______

4. Why does Ben spend a lot of time there? 4. ______________________

____

5. How many books does he read every week? 5. ______________________

____

6. What does he hope? 6. ______________________

7. Who came in? 7. ______________________

8. What was Ben doing? 8. ______________________

9. Why did Anita ask Ben to help her pick out a book in English? 9. ______________________

____

10. What did Ben show her? 10. ______________________

11. How many books did Ben buy? 11. ______________________

12. Why didn't Anita buy any? 12. ______________________

C. Dialogue

DEBBIE: You're late.

BEN: I'm sorry. I had to go to the bookstore.

DEBBIE: How many books did you buy this time?

BEN: Only four.

DEBBIE: Only four! How are you going to find time to read all of them?

BEN: I have to read them for one of my English courses.

DEBBIE: You spend all your money on books.

BEN: Well, I enjoy reading. I learn a lot from books.

DEBBIE: Yes, I learn a lot from them too, but I don't buy them all the time.

BEN: Oh, these are paperbacks. They aren't very expensive.

DEBBIE: You ought to get a job in the bookstore.

BEN: I'm thinking about it.

DEBBIE: Then you'll be able to stay there all day.

BEN: Maybe next year. I don't have to take another science course, so I'll have more time.

Vocabulary Study

A. Study.

1. Bob is doing exercises.

2. Ben showed the exercises to Bob.

3. Bob wants to have bigger arm muscles.

4. He's not as strong as Ben.

5. Bob wants to be a lot stronger than he is now.

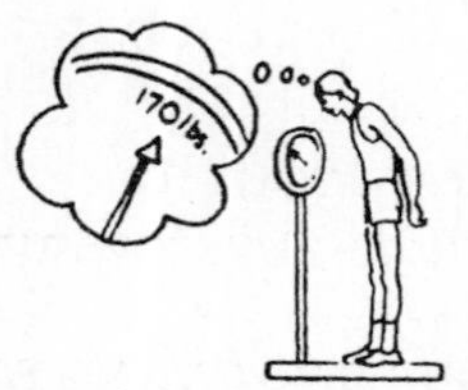

6. He also wants to be heavier.

7. He's lighter than Ben.

8. He can do more push-ups this week than he did last week.

9. He's going to be a lot healthier in a few weeks than he is now.

B. Answer the questions.

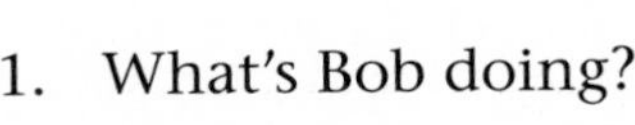

1. What's Bob doing?

1. ______________________

2. Who showed the exercises to Bob?

2. ______________________

____

3. What does Bob want?

3. ______________________

4. Is Bob stronger than Ben?

4. ______________________

5. What does Bob want to be?

5. ______________________

____

6. What else does he want to be?

6. ______________________

____

7. Who's lighter, Bob or Ben? Who's heavier, Bob or Ben?

7. ______________________

____

8. What can Bob do this week?

8. ______________________

____

9. What's he going to be in a few weeks?

9. ______________________

____

C. Study.

THIS WEEK 50° / LAST WEEK 60°

1. It's colder this week than it was last week.

2. This letter is more important than the one you're answering.

3. The weather is warmer than I like it.

4. He's not as heavy as he wants to be.

5. This book isn't as interesting as the one I read last week.

6. He's not as tall as he looks.

> Both comparatives with *than* and comparisons of equality with *as* can be followed by clauses that include a subject and verb of their own in addition to the principal subject and verb of the sentence.

Structure and Pattern Practice

A. Change to the comparative, using the phrase in parentheses.

EXAMPLE

A yard is short. (a meter) — *A yard is shorter than a meter.*

1. Ben is heavy. (Bob) 1. ______
2. Their old office was crowded. (their new one) 2. ______
3. The first field trip was interesting. (the second one) 3. ______
4. He's tall. (I am) 4. ______
5. His car is old. (my car) 5. ______
6. His trip to Chicago is important. (his trip to Los Angeles) 6. ______
7. Their house is large. (it looks) 7. ______
8. This book is difficult. (the one I read last month) 8. ______

B. Change to show comparison of equality, using the phrase in parentheses.

EXAMPLE

He isn't strong. (Ben) — *He isn't as strong as Ben.*

1. I'm not sleepy. (I was last night) 1. ____________________
2. This lesson isn't difficult. (the one we studied last week) 2. ____________________
3. The bus isn't fast. (the subway) 3. ____________________
4. My desk isn't untidy. (her desk) 4. ____________________
5. It isn't warm this month. (it was last month) 5. ____________________
6. Dick isn't careful. (his sister) 6. ____________________
7. My car isn't dirty. (her car) 7. ____________________
8. This field trip isn't interesting. (the one we went on last semester) 8. ____________________

Reading and Conversation Practice

A. Read.

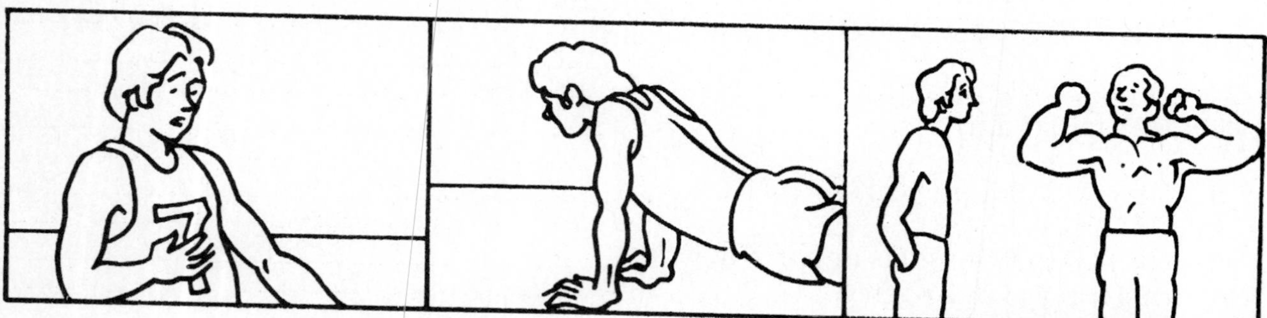

Dan is a little fatter than he wants to be. He's trying to lose some weight. After a month he'll be thinner than he is now. He's on a diet. He's not eating as much as he ate last month. He's more careful about his food. He's not eating a lot of potatoes, bread, and butter. All of them will make him fatter than he is.

Dan is also doing exercises every day. He didn't get enough exercise before because he sat at a desk or in his car all day. Now he runs around the track every day. He also does exercises in his room every morning.

Dan wants to be as healthy as Ben. Ben is healthier and stronger than the other students because he always gets a lot of exercise. He's a better athlete than anyone else in the college. He likes all kinds of sports.

> *To lose* is an irregular verb. The past tense form is *lost*.
>
> Our team loses a lot of football games.
> They lost the football game last week.

B. Answer these questions.

1. Is Dan fatter or thinner than he wants to be? — 1. ______________________
2. What is he trying to do? — 2. ______________________
3. What will he be after a month? — 3. ______________________
4. What is he on? — 4. ______________________
5. Is he eating more than he ate last month? — 5. ______________________
6. What is he more careful about? — 6. ______________________
7. What kind of food is he *not* eating? — 7. ______________________
8. Why isn't he eating them? — 8. ______________________
9. What else is Dan doing every day? — 9. ______________________
10. Why didn't he get enough exercise before? — 10. ______________________
11. What does he do every day now? — 11. ______________________
12. What does he do in his room every morning? — 12. ______________________

13. What does Dan want to be? 13. ______________________

14. Why is Ben healthier and stronger than the other students? 14. ______________________

____

15. Is Ben a good athlete? 15. ______________________

16. What kind of sports does he like? 16. ______________________

C. Dialogue

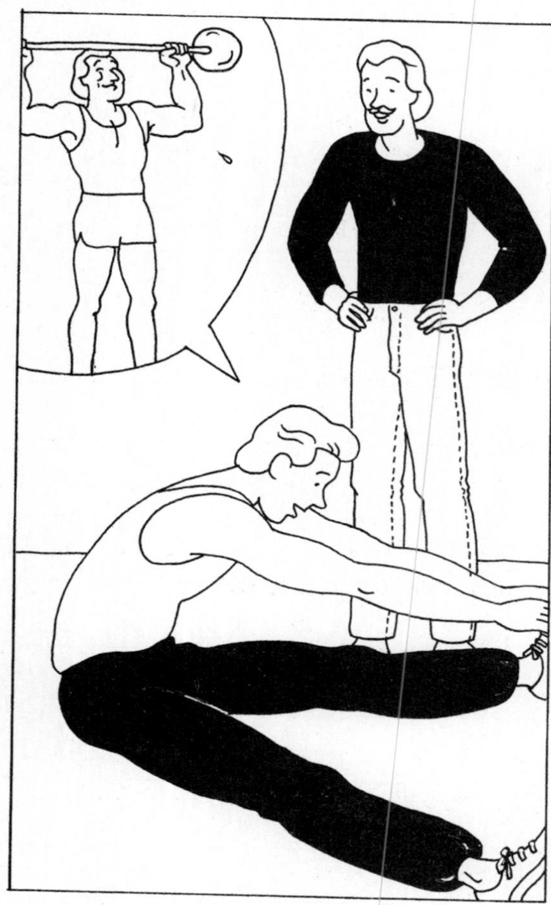

BOB: What are you doing?
DAN: Exercises. I do them every morning.
BOB: Did Ben show them to you?
DAN: Yes, he helped me a lot.
BOB: Lucky Ben. He's a better athlete than we are.
DAN: And a better student too.
BOB: Except in science. He's not as good as we are in chemistry.
DAN: Didn't Ben show you some exercises too?
BOB: Yes, he did. I want to be a little stronger. What about you?
DAN: I'm trying to lose some weight. I'm fatter than I should be.
BOB: Are you going on a diet too?
DAN: I already did. I'm not eating as much as I was.
BOB: Well, go on with your exercises. You won't lose any weight just sitting there.
DAN: Yes, yes, I know.

Additional Vocabulary

arm
athlete
butter
diet (n)
except
fat
(to) lose
muscle
push-up
strong
thin
track (in an athletic field)

LESSON

7

SEVEN

Vocabulary Study

A. Study.

1. Bruce is the most serious person in the office.

2. He works very hard all day.

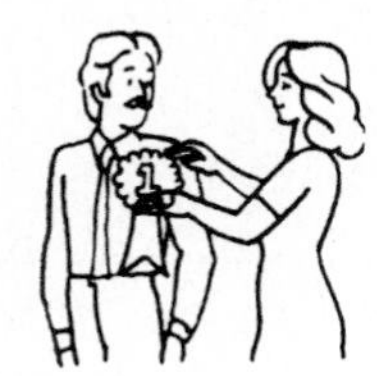

3. He's the hardest worker in the office.

4. Bruce also goes to school at night.

5. He gets the best grades of all the students in his programming class.

6. He's not as good in accounting as in programming.

7. But he doesn't get the worst grades in his accounting class.

8. Bruce wants to become an executive.

9. He's the most ambitious person in the office.

B. Answer the questions.

1. Who's the most serious person in the office?

1. ______________________

____

2. What does he do all day?

2. ______________________

3. What kind of worker is he?

3. ______________________

4. What does Bruce do at night?

4. ______________________

____

5. What kind of grades does he get in his programming class?

5. ______________________

____

6. Is he as good in accounting as in programming?

6. ______________________

____

7. Does he get the worst grades in his accounting class?

7. ______________________

____

8. What does Bruce want to become?

8. ______________________

____

9. Is Bruce more ambitious than the other people in the office?

9. ______________________

____

____

C. Study.

1. That picture is the best that I ever saw.

2. That shirt is the most expensive that I have.

3. These prices are the highest that I can pay.

4. That young woman is the most serious that I know.

5. This book is the most interesting that I ever read.

6. That lecture was the most important that I ever heard.

> Superlatives can also be followed by clauses. Note that these clauses are introduced by *that*.

Structure and Pattern Practice

A. Complete with the superlative form of the adjective in parenthesis.

EXAMPLE

He's ___*the hardest*___ (hard) worker in the office.

1. John wants to be ______________ (healthy) student in the school.
2. The library is ______________ (big) building on the campus.
3. Ben is ______________ (good) athlete in the college.
4. He's ______________ (strong) person on the football team.
5. February is ______________ (short) month of the year.
6. This letter is ______________ (important) that we got yesterday.
7. This course is ______________ (difficult) that I will ever take.
8. That was ______________ (easy) lesson in the book.

B. Change to the superlative, using the phrase in parentheses to complete the sentence.

EXAMPLE

He's a hard worker. (in the office) — *He's the hardest worker in the office.*

1. It's a hot day. (of the year) 1. ____________
2. He's an ambitious worker (in the company) 2. ____________
3. This sweater is expensive. (in the store) 3. ____________
4. Her grades are good. (in the class) 4. ____________
5. She's a good programmer. (that the company has) 5. ____________
6. That was a bad problem. (that I had on my trip) 6. ____________

Reading and Conversation Practice

A. Read.

Ben is the most popular student at Washington College. He's the best athlete and one of the best students in the school. He plays on the football team in the fall and on the baseball team in the spring. He also writes for the college magazine. He spends a lot of time with his friends too.

Ben always seems to be busy with one activity or another, but he still finds time to read and study. His courses in English lit are the easiest for him. The science and math courses are the most difficult. This year he had to take chemistry. He had to study all night to prepare for the final exam. It was the worst exam he ever took, he told everybody. Nevertheless, he got a good grade in the exam. He's just very good at everything he does.

Lit is a short term for *literature*.

B. Answer these questions.

1. Is Ben popular? 1. ______________________
2. Is he a good athlete? 2. ______________________
3. Is he a good student? 3. ______________________
4. What does he do in the fall? 4. ______________________
5. What does he do in the spring? 5. ______________________
6. What else does he do? 6. ______________________
7. Who does he spend a lot of time with? 7. ______________________
8. What does he always seem to be busy with? 8. ______________________
9. What does he still find time to do? 9. ______________________
10. What courses are the easiest for him? 10. ______________________
11. What courses are the most difficult for him? 11. ______________________
12. What did he have to take this year? 12. ______________________
13. What did he have to do to prepare for the final exam? 13. ______________________
14. What did he tell everybody about the exam? 14. ______________________
15. What kind of grade did he get in the exam? 15. ______________________

C. Dialogue

BOB: Did you have a good weekend?
DEBBIE: Well, I studied all day Sunday.
BOB: What about Saturday? Did you go to the baseball game?
DEBBIE: No, I didn't. I went into the city.
BOB: Wasn't it hot?
DEBBIE: It was the hottest day of the year.
BOB: Did you drive in?
DEBBIE: No, I didn't. I took the bus, and it was the most uncomfortable trip that I've ever made.
BOB: Why? What happened?
DEBBIE: The air conditioning in the bus wasn't working.
BOB: Why didn't you just come back home?
DEBBIE: I wanted to go shopping.
BOB: What did you get?
DEBBIE: After all that, I didn't buy anything. The prices at all the stores were the highest that I ever saw.

Additional Vocabulary

activity
air conditioning
ambitious
lit (literature)
nevertheless
person
(to) seem

Vocabulary Study

A. Study.

1. There have been a lot of changes in John Wilson's office.

2. He's given Joan Rossi a promotion.

3. He's made her the office manager.

4. Jane Gold has become John's assistant.

5. They've hired a new word processor to replace Jane.

6. The new word processor's name is Arlene Wong.

7. They may hire more word processors next week.

8. They've had a lot of work recently.

9. Everybody in the office has been very busy.

> *Word processor* is used both for the machine and for the person who operates the machine.

B. Answer the questions.

1. Where have there been a lot of changes?

1. ______________________

2. What has John given Joan Rossi?

2. ______________________

3. What has he made her?

3. ______________________

4. What has Jane Gold become?

4. ______________________

5. Why have they hired a new word processor?

5. ______________________

____

6. What's the new word processor's name?

ARLENE WONG

6. ______________________

____

7. What may they do next week?

7. ______________________

____

8. Have they had much work recently?

8. ______________________

____

9. Who's been very busy?

9. ______________________

____

C. Study.

1. They've drunk all their milk. There isn't a drop left.

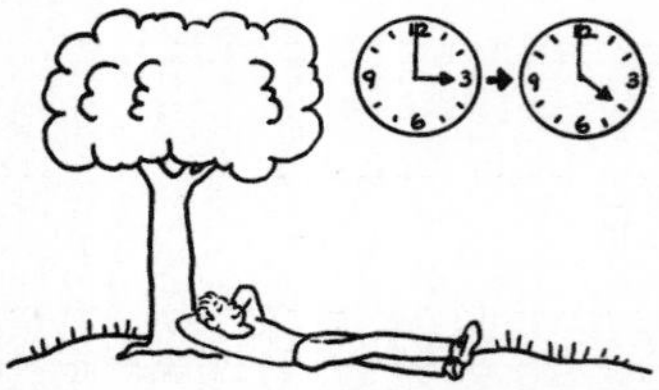

2. He's lain under that tree for an hour.

SCORE

US	80	65	72
THEM	12	18	5

3. Our team hasn't lost a game yet. We're going to be the champions.

4. We aren't ready for dinner. I haven't set the table yet.

5. He hasn't swept the floor yet. There's dust everywhere.

6. Our team has won all of its football games this year.

> The sentences above use the past participle forms of irregular verbs that do not appear in books 1, 2, or 3. The past participle forms of other irregular verbs are given on pages 151–52 of book 3. The principal parts of *to set (the table)* are *set-set-set*.

Structure and Pattern Practice

A. Change to the present perfect. Change the time expression to *recently*.

EXAMPLE

They had a lot of work last month. *They've had a lot of work recently.*

1. It rained a lot last month. 1. ______________________
2. He did a lot of exercises last week. 2. ______________________
3. I wrote some letters yesterday. 3. ______________________
4. The teacher gave a lot of homework last semester. 4. ______________________
5. His father taught him a lot about carpentry last summer. 5. ______________________
6. He went on several business trips last month. 6. ______________________

B. Change to the negative.

EXAMPLE

The store has opened. — *The store hasn't opened.*

1. He's handed in his report. 1. ______________________
2. She's looked at the schedule. 2. ______________________
3. I've seen that picture before. 3. ______________________
4. There have been a lot of fires this year. 4. ______________________ ______________________
5. We've started the new semester. 5. ______________________
6. You've been very good to me. 6. ______________________

C. Change first to affirmative questions and then to negative questions.

EXAMPLE

They've had a lot of work recently. — *Have they had a lot of work recently?* *Haven't they had a lot of work recently?*

1. He's gone out to lunch. 1. ______________________ ______________________
2. I've seen that picture. (you) 2. ______________________ ______________________
3. The picture has started. 3. ______________________ ______________________
4. They've put her in charge of the office. 4. ______________________ ______________________
5. She's cleaned up her room. 5. ______________________ ______________________
6. We've been away for a month. (you) 6. ______________________ ______________________

E. Complete with the appropriate attached questions.

EXAMPLE

He's swept the floor, *hasn't he?*

1. She hasn't bought anything, ______________?
2. You haven't answered my question, ______________?
3. You've finished your term paper, ______________?
4. They've hired a lot of new people, ______________?
5. She hasn't talked to her professor, ______________?
6. He's assigned a lot of homework, ______________?
7. You haven't ever worked in an office before, ______________?
8. She's paid her tuition, ______________?

F. Complete with *for* or *since* and the phrase in parentheses.

EXAMPLE

I haven't seen my adviser. (two months) *I haven't seen my adviser for two months.*

1. They haven't gone skiing. (March) 1. ______________________________
2. They haven't had a dance. (June) 2. ______________________________
3. They've been very busy. (the last three weeks) 3. ______________________________
4. She's been the office manager. (last Monday) 4. ______________________________
5. Bob has had a part-time job. (September) 5. ______________________________
6. I've attended Washington College. (two semesters) 6. ______________________________
7. Akira hasn't gone home. (two years) 7. ______________________________
8. She's been absent. (Tuesday) 8. ______________________________

Reading and Conversation Practice

A. Read.

The winter semester at Washington College has ended. The students have taken their final exams. Now they have a week's vacation before the spring semester. The weather has been very pleasant for the first weekend of the vacation. It's been warm and it hasn't rained much.

Several of the students have gone away for the week. Akira has gone to New York. He wants to have some fun because he's studied very hard this year. He's planning to do a lot of sightseeing in New York.

Bob has also left for the week. He's gone to visit his family again. This time he's invited Ben to come with him. Ben hasn't visited Bob's family before. They'll eat a lot and just rest and have a quiet time.

B. Answer these questions.

1. What has ended?	1. ________________
2. What have the students taken?	2. ________________
3. What do they have now?	3. ________________
4. How has the weather been?	4. ________________
5. What have several of the students done?	5. ________________ ________________
6. Where has Akira gone?	6. ________________
7. Why does he want to have some fun?	7. ________________ ________________
8. What's he planning to do?	8. ________________
9. Who else has gone away?	9. ________________
10. Where has Bob gone?	10. ________________

11. What has he invited Ben to do? 11. ______________________

12. Has Ben visited Bob's family before? 12. ______________________

____

13. What will they do? 13. ______________________

C. Dialogue

DEBBIE: Hi, Dan. Where have you been?
DAN: At the library. I'm trying to study over the vacation.
DEBBIE: Come and sit down for a minute or two.
DAN: Thank you. It's peaceful here.
DEBBIE: Yes, the campus seems quiet today.
DAN: Yes, it sure does. Just about everybody's left for the week.
DEBBIE: Where's Akira?
DAN: He's gone to New York to do some sightseeing.
DEBBIE: Has Bob gone home?
DAN: Yes, he has, and Ben's gone with him.
DEBBIE: I'm happy just to stay here. The campus is beautiful in the spring.
DAN: Yes, and the weather's been wonderful this week.
DEBBIE: Have you really been able to do any studying?
DAN: Well, I've done a little anyway.

Additional Vocabulary

champion
drop (n)
dust (n)
everywhere
(to) invite
peaceful
quiet
(to) replace
(to) set

Vocabulary Study

A. Study.

1. Akira had planned his trip to New York for a long time.

2. He'd heard about what to see in New York.

3. He'd read several guide books before he went.

4. He'd made a reservation at a hotel.

5. He'd sent for theater and concert tickets.

6. Akira got back to the campus Sunday night.

7. He told his friends that he'd had a very good time.

8. He said that he'd done a lot of sightseeing.

9. He said that he'd liked the boat trip around New York best of all.

B. Answer the questions.

1. What had Akira planned for a long time?

1. ____________________
____

2. What had he heard about?

2. ____________________
____

3. What had he read before he went?

3. ____________________
____

4. What kind of reservation had he made?

4. ____________________
____

5. What kind of tickets had he sent for?

5. ____________________
____

6. When did Akira get back to the campus?

6. ______________________

7. What did he tell his friends?

7. ______________________

8. What did he say that he'd done?

8. ______________________

9. What did he say that he'd liked best?

9. ______________________

C. Study.

1. Which sport do you like best?
   I like baseball best.

2. Which city did he like best?
   He liked San Francisco best.

3. Which subject do you like best?
   I like math best.

4. Which season do you like best?
   I like spring best.

5. Which field trip did the students like best?
   They liked the first one best.

6. Which car does he like best?
   He likes the new one best.

Structure and Pattern Practice

A. Change these sentences so that they begin with *He said that*. Change the past tense to the past perfect.

EXAMPLE

He had a good time. — *He said that he'd had a good time.*

1. He lost his book. 1. ______________________
2. The weather was good. 2. ______________________
3. He gave his assistant a better job. 3. ______________________
4. Sue took a trip to New York. 4. ______________________
5. Sue planned her trip for a long time. 5. ______________________
6. The exams were very difficult. 6. ______________________
7. He saw a baseball game. 7. ______________________
8. There were a lot of people on the bus. 8. ______________________

B. Change first to affirmative questions and then to negative questions.

EXAMPLE

She'd had a good time. — *Had she had a good time?*

Hadn't she had a good time?

1. It had rained during the night. — 1. ______ / ______
2. She'd gotten a promotion. — 2. ______ / ______
3. They'd hired more word processors. — 3. ______ / ______
4. I'd read the guide book. (you) — 4. ______ / ______
5. There had been a dance in the gym. — 5. ______ / ______
6. We'd sent for tickets to the concert. (you) — 6. ______ / ______

C. Change to the negative.

EXAMPLE

He'd seen the picture. — *He hadn't seen the picture.*

1. She'd filed all the letters. — 1. ______
2. I'd eaten a hamburger at the cafeteria. — 2. ______ / ______
3. You'd handed in your homework. — 3. ______
4. We'd visited a factory before. — 4. ______
5. They'd made some changes in the factory. — 5. ______ / ______

Reading and Conversation Practice

A. Read.

Dan missed his Spanish class yesterday. He'd been up late the night before. They'd shown his favorite old movie on television. He'd stayed up until two o'clock because he wanted to see the end of the picture.

In the morning he didn't hear his alarm clock. His mother finally called him because he hadn't come downstairs. He dressed and washed in a hurry. He didn't eat any breakfast.

He ran all the way to the bus stop. Then he remembered that he hadn't picked up his briefcase. He'd put his books and his homework in the briefcase the night before. He went back home to get it. By that time the bus had left. When he finally got to the campus, the Spanish class had ended.

B. Answer these questions.

1. What did Dan miss yesterday? 1. ______________________
2. Why hadn't he gone to bed early the night before? 2. ______________________ ______________________
3. How late had he stayed up? 3. ______________________
4. Why had he stayed up that late? 4. ______________________
5. Did he hear his alarm clock in the morning? 5. ______________________ ______________________
6. Why did his mother finally call him? 6. ______________________ ______________________
7. How did he dress and wash? 7. ______________________
8. Did he eat a big breakfast? 8. ______________________
9. Did he walk to the bus stop? 9. ______________________

10. Then what did he remember? 10. ________________

11. Why did he need his briefcase? 11. ________________

12. Why did he go back? 12. ________________

13. What had happened by that time? 13. ________________

____

14. What had happened when he finally got to the campus? 14. ________________

____

C. Dialogue

BOB: Have you seen Akira?
DEBBIE: Yes, I have. He's going to stay home today. He wants to rest a little.
BOB: When did he get back?
DEBBIE: Late last night.
BOB: Did you talk to him?
DEBBIE: Yes, for a couple of minutes. He was very tired.
BOB: Did he have a good time?
DEBBIE: Yes, wonderful. He said that he'd enjoyed every minute of the trip.
BOB: What did he see?
DEBBIE: He said that he'd seen absolutely everything.
BOB: How did he know what everything was?
DEBBIE: Oh, he'd read a lot of guide books before he left.
BOB: What did he like best, did he tell you?
DEBBIE: Yes, he loved all the shows and concerts.

Additional Vocabulary

absolutely
alarm (clock)
briefcase
end (n)
favorite
guide (book)
reservation
season
show (n)

LESSON

10 REVIEW

TEN

Structure and Pattern Practice

A. Change to the comparative, using the phrase in parentheses.

EXAMPLE

Ben is strong. (the other men) — *Ben is stronger than the other men.*

1. My coat was expensive. (my shirt) 1. ____________________
2. New York is large. (Chicago) 2. ____________________
3. Los Angeles is small. (New York) 3. ____________________
4. The new building is convenient. (the old building) 4. ____________________
5. The exam was long. (the one we had last month) 5. ____________________

B. Change to the superlative, using the phrase in parentheses.

EXAMPLE

He's a hard worker. (in the office) — *He's the hardest worker in the office.*

1. Bruce is a good student. (in the programming class) 1. ____________________
2. New York is a big city. (in the United States) 2. ____________________
3. That was a bad exam. (I took last semester) 3. ____________________
4. It was an uncomfortable hotel. (I stayed at on our vacation) 4. ____________________

C. Change to the present perfect. Change the time expression to *recently*.

EXAMPLE

They hired a lot of clerks last month. *They've hired a lot of clerks recently.*

1. It rained several times this week. 1. ______
2. She got another promotion last week. 2. ______
3. She talked to a lot of students yesterday. 3. ______
4. We had a lot of exams last month. 4. ______
5. The professor gave us a lot of homework last semester. 5. ______
6. She went to the lab several times last week. 6. ______
7. He got several packages last week. 7. ______
8. You invited me to visit you last year. 8. ______

D. Change these sentences so that they begin with *She said that*. Change the past tense to the past perfect.

EXAMPLE

He corrected the mistakes. *She said that he'd corrected the mistakes.*

1. She made a reservation at a hotel. 1. ______
2. She went to the language lab. 2. ______
3. They began a new lesson. 3. ______
4. We won the game. 4. ______
5. He forgot his briefcase. 5. ______
6. He wrote some letters. 6. ______
7. His car broke down. 7. ______
8. She sent for theater tickets. 8. ______

E. Change to the negative.

EXAMPLE

She's seen her professor. *She hasn't seen her professor.*

1. We've filed all the letters. 1. ______
2. She'd visited New York before. 2. ______
3. The professor has read all the term papers. 3. ______
4. He's lost a lot of weight. 4. ______
5. We'd been on a field trip before. 5. ______
6. She's made a hotel reservation. 6. ______

F. Change first to affirmative questions and then to negative questions.

EXAMPLE

She's seen her adviser. *Has she seen her adviser?*

Hasn't she seen her adviser?

1. We've seen his pictures. (you) 1. ______
2. He's found his briefcase. 2. ______
3. She'd finished her homework. 3. ______
4. They'd replaced the word processors. 4. ______
5. I'd heard my alarm clock. (you) 5. ______
6. The bus had been very uncomfortable. 6. ______

Reading and Conversation Practice

A. Read.

Arlene Wong has worked in John Wilson's office for a month. All the word processors have been very busy because there's a lot of work. Joan Rossi hasn't had time to check Arlene's work, but Arlene is a very careful worker. She learned to use a word processor in high school. She always checks her own work. John has begun to give Arlene more important work.

Arlene had never had a job before. She'd been a college student. She left school because she needed to make some money. She's planning to return to college after she's worked for a year. She's planning to major in sociology.

Arlene always has a book in her purse. She reads on the subway every morning and evening. She also reads during her lunch hour. The other people in the office think that she's a little too serious.

B. Answer these questions.

1. How long has Arlene Wong worked in John Wilson's office? 1. ______________________
2. Why have all the word processors been busy? 2. ______________________
3. Why hasn't Joan Rossi checked Arlene's work? 3. ______________________
4. What kind of worker is Arlene? 4. ______________________
5. Where did she learn to use a word processor? 5. ______________________
6. What has John begun to do? 6. ______________________
7. How many jobs had Arlene had before? 7. ______________________

8. What had she been? 8. ______________________________

9. Why did she leave school? 9. ______________________________

10. When is she planning to return to college? 10. ______________________________

____

11. What's she going to major in? 11. ______________________________

12. Where does she always have a book? 12. ______________________________

____

13. What does she do during her lunch hour? 13. ______________________________

____

14. What do the other people in the office think about her? 14. ______________________________

____

C. Dialogue

ANITA: What do you have there?
AKIRA: They're pictures of New York.
ANITA: Oh, may I see them?
AKIRA: Yes, go ahead, look at them.
ANITA: They're really good! Who took them?
AKIRA: They're *my* pictures. *I* took them.
ANITA: I thought you didn't like your camera.
AKIRA: I bought a new camera when I was in New York. It's much better than my old one.
ANITA: Yes, I can see that. These are the best pictures of New York that I've ever seen.
AKIRA: Thank you, Anita. That's very nice of you.
ANITA: You should show them to everybody.
AKIRA: Well, I have shown them to a few people.
ANITA: You're lucky. I've never been able to take good pictures.
AKIRA: You probably just don't take as much time with them as you should.

Vocabulary Study

A. Study.

1. Dan always forgets things.

2. He writes notes to himself.

3. Sometimes he reminds himself about his schedule for the day.

4. Other times he reminds himself about his homework.

5. The notes themselves are very short.

6. Dan puts the notes on his bathroom mirror.

7. He shaves every morning.

8. When he looks at himself in the mirror, he sees the notes.

9. Dan wants to teach himself to remember things better.

B. Answer the questions.

1. Does Dan always remember things?

1. ____________________

2. What does he write?

2. ____________________

3. What does he remind himself about sometimes?

3. ____________________

4. What does he remind himself about other times?

4. ____________________

5. Are the notes themselves very long?

5. ____________________

6. Where does he put the notes?

6. ______________________

____

7. What does he do every morning?

7. ______________________

____

8. When does he see the notes?

8. ______________________

____

9. What does Dan want to do?

THINGS TO REMEMBER

9. ______________________

____

C. Study.

1. The notes help him to remember things.
The notes help him remember things.

2. The tape recorder helps her to practice pronunciation.
The tape recorder helps her practice pronunciation.

3. He helped his father to build a garage.
He helped his father build a garage.

4. Her mother helped her to clean up her room.
Her mother helped her clean up her room.

5. She's helping me to write my term paper.
   She's helping me write my term paper.

6. I'm helping the children to paint their room.
   I'm helping the children paint their room.

> *Help* can be followed either by the infinitive or by the simple form of the verb without *to*.

Structure and Pattern Practice

A. Complete these sentences with the correct reflexive pronoun.

EXAMPLE

She bought *herself* a new hat.

1. Bob, don't talk about ____________ all the time.
2. He always cuts ____________ when he shaves.
3. You can listen to ____________ on this tape recorder.
4. Joan Rossi never talks about ____________.
5. I'm going to get ____________ a cup of coffee.
6. We can hear ____________ on these tape recorders.
7. You boys are always looking at ____________ in the mirror.
8. She must remind ____________ about her appointment.
9. He didn't hurt ____________ in the accident.
10. You children can make your beds ____________ .

B. Substitute *by* and the appropriate intensive pronoun for *alone* or *without help*.

EXAMPLE

Debbie is sitting over there alone. *Debbie is sitting over there by herself.*

1. You children can't go swimming alone. 1. ______________________

2. He finished the term paper without help. 2. ______________________

3. Anita is learning the new words without help. 3. ______________________

4. Why do you boys like to study alone? 4. ______________________

5. The book is sitting all alone in the middle of the desk. 5. ______________________

6. I want to go for a ride in the country alone. 6. ______________________

7. Bob, you can't build a garage without help. 7. ______________________

8. The girl and the boy were playing ball alone. 8. ______________________

9. I can answer this letter without help. 9. ______________________

10. You can't paint the house without help. 10. ______________________

Reading and Conversation Practice

A. Read.

Anita can speak English very well now. Last year she was in a special English class for foreign students. In addition to the regular class, she went to the lab for an hour every day. There are a lot of tape recorders in the language lab. The students can listen to themselves. When the students hear their mistakes, they can correct themselves.

Anita still doesn't write as well as she speaks. Sometimes she doesn't understand a word or two. She has a dictionary on her desk. When she sees a new word, she looks it up right away. Then she repeats it to herself. She still goes to the lab too. The students can use the lab by themselves. Anita writes sentences of her own with the new words. When she reads them into the tape recorder, she can hear herself.

B. Answer these questions.

1. How is Anita's English now?	1. ______________________
2. What kind of class was she in last year?	2. ______________________ ______________________
3. What did she do in addition to the regular class?	3. ______________________ ______________________
4. What is there in the language lab?	4. ______________________ ______________________
5. Who can the students listen to?	5. ______________________
6. What can they do when they hear their mistakes?	6. ______________________ ______________________
7. Does Anita write English well?	7. ______________________
8. Does she understand every word?	8. ______________________
9. What does she do when she sees a new word?	9. ______________________ ______________________

10. What does she do then? 10. ______________________

11. Where does she still go? 11. ______________________

12. Do the students need a teacher when they use the lab? 12. ______________________
____

13. What does Anita write? 13. ______________________

14. What happens when she reads them into the tape recorder? 14. ______________________
____

C. Dialogue

BOB: What are all those pieces of paper on the bathroom mirror?
DAN: Oh, those? They're just little notes.
BOB: Notes? What are they for?
DAN: I write them to myself.
BOB: Well, why?
DAN: I use them to remind myself about things.
BOB: Can't you remember things without notes?
DAN: I forget stuff all the time.
BOB: Aren't you trying to do anything about it?
DAN: Well, I write myself these notes.
BOB: No, I mean something to improve your memory.
DAN: I keep trying to teach myself to remember things better.
BOB: What do you do about exams?
DAN: Oh, I don't forget that kind of thing. Errands, dates, telephone numbers—those are the things I forget.

Additional Vocabulary

bathroom
(to) look up
memory
number
(to) paint
(to) practice
pronunciation
(to) remind
(to) repeat
(to) shave

LESSON

12

TWELVE

Vocabulary Study

A. Study.

1. Today is the last day of the semester.

2. There's going to be a graduation ceremony in the gym.

3. The gym is the only building that's large enough for the ceremony.

4. The students who are going to graduate are already inside the gym.

5. The people who are going to watch the ceremony are entering the gym now.

6. Most of them are the parents and friends of the students who are going to graduate.

7. They'll listen to a speech by the student who received the highest grade in the class.

8. The students who graduate will receive a diploma.

9. After the ceremony, the students will spend the rest of the day with their families and friends.

B. Answer the questions.

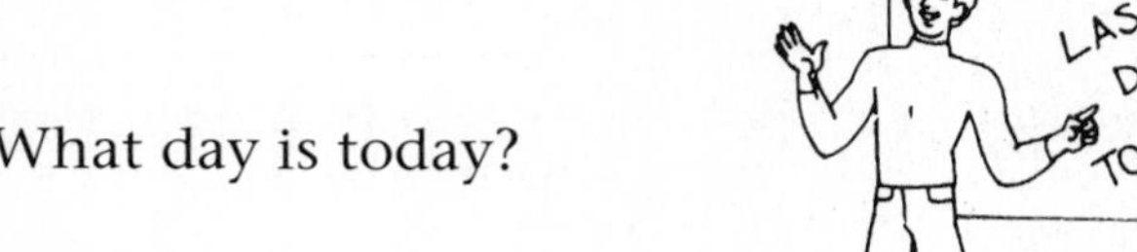

1. What day is today?

1. ______________________

2. What is there going to be in the gym?

2. ______________________

____

3. Why is the ceremony in the gym?

3. ______________________

____

4. Where are the students who are going to graduate?

4. ______________________

____

5. Who is entering the gym now?

5. ______________________

____

6. Who are the people entering the gym?

6. ______________________

____

7. Who will give a speech?

7. ______________________

8. What will the students who graduate receive?

8. ______________________

____

9. What will the students do after the ceremony?

9. ______________________

____

C. Study.

1. I wrote a few of the letters.
The boss wrote the rest of them.

2. He took some of the packages to the post office today.
He'll take the rest of them tomorrow.

3. Half of the students were at the graduation ceremony.
The rest of them stayed home.

4. I can do the first two exercises.
I can't do the rest of them.

5. They did some of the experiments this semester. They'll do the rest of them next semester.

6. I drank some of the milk. The children drank the rest of it.

Structure and Pattern Practice

A. Change *who* or *which* to *that.*

EXAMPLE

I haven't met the woman who I saw in your office. — *I haven't met the woman that I saw in your office.*

1. He didn't catch the plane which he'd planned to take. 1. ______

2. He hasn't called the young woman who he met at the dance. 2. ______

3. They didn't do the experiment which they'd prepared for. 3. ______

4. The sandwiches which Bob made tasted wonderful. 4. ______

5. The student who she's talking to is going to graduate this semester. 5. ______

6. The woman who she replaced has gotten a better job. 6. ______

7. The experiment which they did last week was dangerous. 7. ______

B. Combine these sentences, using *who* to connect them. The second sentence should become an adjective clause.

EXAMPLE

The people are entering the gym. They're going to watch the ceremony.

The people who are going to watch the ceremony are entering the gym.

1. They don't like the professor. He gave them that difficult assignment.

1. ______________________________

2. I haven't met the woman. She replaced Joan Rossi.

2. ______________________________

3. He gave good grades to the students. They finished all the experiments.

3. ______________________________

4. The students worked on Saturday morning. They were on the committee to clean up the gym.

4. ______________________________

5. The students ran to the gym. They had been out on the track.

5. ______________________________

6. The students got wet when it began to rain. They were playing tennis.

6. ______________________________

7. I know some of the musicians. They played in the concert last night.

7. ______________________________

8. She'd never seen the employee. He was waiting to talk to Mr.Wilson.

8. ______________________________

C. Combine these sentences, using *that* to connect them. The second sentence should become an adjective clause.

EXAMPLE

I haven't seen the letters. The boss wrote them yesterday. — *I haven't seen the letters that the boss wrote yesterday.*

1. The book is very difficult. We're using it this year. — 1. ______________________

2. I can't find the books. I got them from the library. — 2. ______________________

3. He's going to hand in the term paper. He finished it last night. — 3. ______________________

4. She just bought the dress. She's wearing it today. — 4. ______________________

5. The exam was important. He missed it. — 5. ______________________

Reading and Conversation Practice

A. Read.

The students who live in the dormitory are getting ready for the summer vacation. Bob is packing his bags. He wants to catch a bus which leaves at two o'clock. Akira is helping him. Akira isn't going to take a vacation because he's going to attend classes this summer. He's going to take care of the things that Bob doesn't want to take home with him. Bob is trying to select the books and clothes that he won't need during the summer. Akira is putting everything that Bob isn't taking with him into the closet.

Ben is going to drive Bob to the bus station, which is a long way from the campus. He's gone to a filling station to get gas. Bob is worried because he may miss the bus that he wants to catch.

Now Ben has come back from the gasoline station and he's blowing the car horn. Bob and Akira run downstairs. Bob says goodbye to Akira. Then he gets in the car, and Ben drives him to the bus station.

B. Answer these questions.

1. Which students are getting ready for the summer vacation? 1. ______________________________

____

2. What is Bob doing? 2. ______________________________

3. What does he want to catch? 3. ______________________________

4. Who is helping Bob? 4. ______________________________

5. Why isn't Akira going to take a vacation? 5. ______________________________

____

6. What is Akira going to take care of? 6. ______________________________

7. What is Bob trying to select? 7. ______________________________

8. What is Akira putting into the closet? 8. ______________________________

____

9. What is Ben going to do? 9. ______________________________

10. Is the bus station near the campus or a long way from it? 10. ______________________________

____

11. Where has Ben gone? 11. ______________________________

12. Why is Bob worried? 12. ______________________________

13. Where has Ben come back from now? 13. ______________________________

____

14. What is he doing? 14. ______________________________

15. What do Bob and Akira do? 15. ______________________________

16. What does Bob say to Akira? 16. ______________________________

17. What happens then? 17. ______________________________

C. Dialogue

DEBBIE: Do you have time for a cup of coffee?

BOB: I don't know. The cafeteria looks pretty crowded.

DEBBIE: It's all the people who went to the graduation.

BOB: Did you go?

DEBBIE: Oh yes, I went! I wanted to hear the speech that Paul gave.

BOB: Oh, he's a friend of yours, isn't he?

DEBBIE: Yes, I've known him for years.

BOB: Didn't he go to the same high school that you did?

DEBBIE: Yes, he did. There he is now! I want to congratulate him.

BOB: Look at all the people who are with him!

DEBBIE: Those are his parents who are sitting next to him. I'll just go over and say hello.

BOB: I ought to get on back to the dormitory. I have to catch a bus that leaves at two o'clock.

DEBBIE: What time is it now?

BOB: It's one thirty already.

DEBBIE: I'll only be a minute, I promise. Then I'll walk over to the dorm with you.

Additional Vocabulary

ceremony
closet
(to) congratulate
diploma
dorm (dormitory)
(to) enter
filling station
(to) graduate
graduation
(to) pack
pretty (intensifier)
(to) receive
(the) rest (of)
(to) select
speech
worried (adj)

LESSON

13

THIRTEEN

Vocabulary Study

A. Study.

1. Akira wasn't as busy as he expected to be this summer.

2. He wanted to take four courses.

3. He was only allowed to take three.

4. Summer students aren't permitted to take more than three courses.

5. The courses that he took are required for his engineering program.

6. Not all his time was spent reading and studying for his classes.

7. He had some free time to play tennis.

8. Finally he was asked by Anita to help the foreign student program.

9. Anita had stayed over the summer to work with the new foreign students.

10. Akira was glad to help her organize activities for the students.

B. Answer the questions.

1. How busy was Akira this summer?

1. ____________________________

____

2. How many courses did he want to take?

2. ____________________________

____

3. How many was he allowed to take?

3. ____________________________

____

4. How many courses are summer students permitted to take?

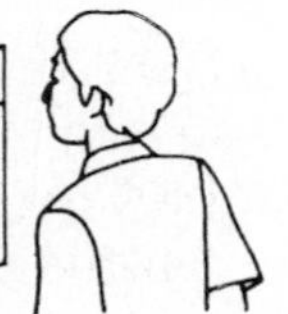

4. ____________________________

____

____

5. What are the courses that he took required for?

5. ______________________________

6. Was all this time spent reading and studying?

6. ______________________________

7. What did he have some free time to do?

7. ______________________________

8. What was he finally asked to do by Anita?

8. ______________________________

9. Why had Anita stayed over the summer?

9. ______________________________

10. What was Akira glad to help her do?

10. ______________________________

C. Study.

1. Many people in Hawaii and California speak Chinese.
Chinese is spoken by many people in Hawaii and California.

2. They require the engineering students to take several lab courses.
The engineering students are required to take several lab courses.

3. They don't allow the summer students to take more than three courses.
   The summer students aren't allowed to take more than three courses.

4. They transferred him to the accounting section.
   He was transferred to the accounting section.

5. The professor congratulated the students who graduated.
   The students who graduated were congratulated by the professor.

6. The teacher didn't correct the homework.
   The homework wasn't corrected by the teacher.

Structure and Pattern Practice

A. Change to the passive. Do not change the tense. Do not use a prepositional phrase to express the agent if the subject of the original sentence is a pronoun.

EXAMPLE

They found the letter in the wastebasket. *The letter was found in the wastebasket.*

1. They organized many activities for the foreign students. 1. ______________________
2. The students decorated the gym. 2. ______________________
3. The clerks addressed all the envelopes. 3. ______________________
4. They speak Spanish in Venezuela. 4. ______________________
5. They hire new employees every month. 5. ______________________

B. Change to the active. If no agent is expressed in the original sentence, use *they* as the subject.

EXAMPLE

He was given a promotion. — *They gave him a promotion.*

1. The lab courses are taught by an engineer. 1. ____________________
2. She was required to study English. 2. ____________________
3. The meeting was held on Monday. 3. ____________________
4. They were helped by the professor. 4. ____________________
5. He was warned not to arrive late. 5. ____________________

C. Change to the passive. Do not change the tense. Do not use a prepositional phrase to express the agent if the subject of the original sentence is a pronoun.

EXAMPLE

Did a careless worker cause the accident? — *Was the accident caused by a careless worker?*

1. Do they require these courses for graduation? 1. ____________________
2. Does the teacher explain all new words? 2. ____________________
3. Do some people speak Spanish in New York? 3. ____________________
4. Do they allow the students to talk in class? 4. ____________________
5. Did they allow you to miss the exam? 5. ____________________

Reading and Conversation Practice

A. Read.

The summer English classes at the college are open to the general public. Many of the summer students aren't planning to attend classes in the fall. May Wan is a Chinese woman who has enrolled in a beginning class. She speaks only a few words of English.

May and her husband, Leo, own a small gift shop in town. The Wans—husband and wife and three children—live in an apartment above the store. Leo works in the store ten or twelve hours a day six days a week selling merchandise from Japan and Hong Kong. He wants May to help him in the store, but she can't because she doesn't know enough English.

May is having a hard time in the class. She finds English pronunciation difficult, and she doesn't always understand the teacher. However, her husband helps her with her homework every night. He wants her to be able to work with him as soon as possible.

B. Answer these questions.

1. Are the summer English classes open only to students at the college? 1. ______________________
2. Are all the summer students planning to attend classes in the fall? 2. ______________________
3. Who is May Wan? 3. ______________________
4. How much English does she speak? 4. ______________________
5. What do the Wans own? 5. ______________________
6. Where do they live? 6. ______________________
7. How many people are there in the Wan family? 7. ______________________
8. What hours does Leo Wan work? 8. ______________________
9. What does he sell in the store? 9. ______________________

10. Why can't May help him in the store? 10. ______________________

____

11. How is May doing in class? 11. ______________________

12. What does she find difficult about English? 12. ______________________

____

13. What does Leo do every night? 13. ______________________

14. What does he want her to be able to do? 14. ______________________

____

C. Dialogue

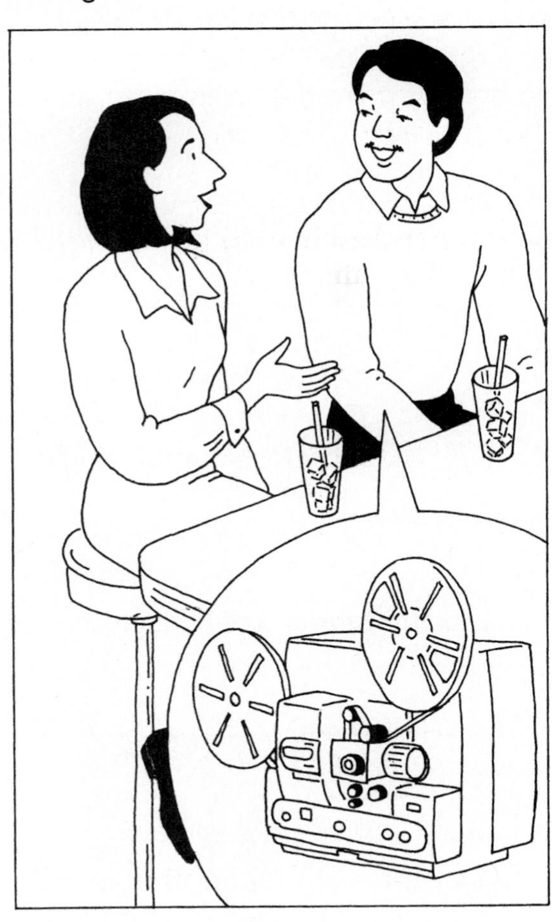

AKIRA: What can we do for our students now?

ANITA: I don't know. We've already had a picnic and a dance.

AKIRA: What about some field trips?

ANITA: I'm afraid we'd lose one or two of the students.

AKIRA: What about some movies then?

ANITA: Movies? You mean educational movies?

AKIRA: No, no, just regular movies, entertainment.

ANITA: In English?

AKIRA: Yes, sure. What else?

ANITA: Do you think the students would understand enough to enjoy them?

AKIRA: We could meet afterwards to talk about them.

ANITA: It's possible. They'd probably learn something.

AKIRA: And have a good time too.

ANITA: All right, we'll try it.

Additional Vocabulary

above
afterwards
(to) allow
beginning
educational
(to) enroll
(to) expect
general
gift
however
merchandise
(to) organize
(to) own
(to) permit
public
(to) require
(to) transfer

Vocabulary Study

A. Study.

1. The summer classes will be finished on Friday.

2. The final exams have already been given.

3. The grades have been mailed out to the students.

4. The dormitory and the cafeteria will be closed tomorrow.

5. The fall semester won't begin for another month.

6. Most of the students have already gone home.

7. Akira has just said goodbye to Anita.

8. Akira is going to take a trip to Washington until school begins again.

9. Anita is going to visit friends in Puerto Rico.

B. Answer the questions.

1. What will happen on Friday?

1. ______________________

2. Do the students still have to take their final exams?

2. ______________________

3. Have the students received their grades?

3. ______________________

4. Are the dormitory and the cafeteria still open?

4. ______________________

5. When will they be open again?

5. ______________________

6. When will the fall semester begin?

6. ______________________

____

7. Where are most of the students?

7. ______________________

____

8. What has Akira just done?

8. ______________________

9. What is Akira going to do?

9. ______________________

10. What is Anita going to do?

10. ______________________

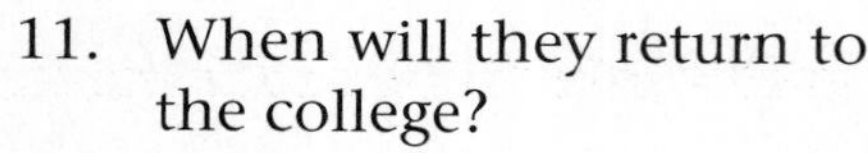

11. When will they return to the college?

11. ______________________

____

C. Study.

1. The work on the computer has been completed.

2. All the merchandise from Hong Kong had been sold before inventory was taken.

3. The meeting will be held in a motel.

4. Everyone in the office is going to be asked to attend the meeting.

5. He can't be permitted to take more than three courses.

6. He should be transferred to a more responsible job.

Structure and Pattern Practice

A. Change to the passive. Do not change the tense. Do not use a prepositional phrase to express the agent if the subject of the original sentence is a pronoun.

EXAMPLE

They have transferred him to a new job. *He has been transferred to a new job.*

1. They may require her to study math. 1. ______
2. They should allow him to take four courses. 2. ______
3. They won't open the cafeteria until September. 3. ______
4. They have assigned the children to a new school. 4. ______
5. They hadn't given the final exams. 5. ______
6. They can hold the meeting in a motel. 6. ______

B. Change to the active. If no agent is expressed in the original sentence, use *they* as the subject.

EXAMPLE

He is going to be transferred. *They are going to transfer him.*

1. The work must be finished today. 1. ______________________
2. The problem can be explained by the teacher. 2. ______________________
3. The letters will be delivered soon. 3. ______________________
4. The grades should be mailed out soon. 4. ______________________
5. All that work can be done by a computer. 5. ______________________
6. Her schedule has been checked by her professor. 6. ______________________

C. Change to the passive. Do not change the tense. Do not use a prepositional phrase to express the agent if the subject of the original sentence is a pronoun.

EXAMPLE

Will they mail out the grades? *Will the grades be mailed out?*

1. Can they hold the dance in a hotel? 1. ______________________
2. Are they going to use the computer for inventory? 2. ______________________
3. Had his assistant told him about the meeting? 3. ______________________
4. Has the professor seen her schedule? 4. ______________________
5. Will they hold a meeting for the foreign students? 5. ______________________
6. Should they improve the special English program? 6. ______________________

Reading and Conversation Practice

A. Read.

Ursula is a German woman who is married to an American army sergeant named Frank Mason. They met each other when he was stationed in Germany, but a year ago he was transferred to an army base in the United States. The base is only a few miles from Washington College.

Ursula spoke enough English to be put in the advanced class in the summer English program. English usually isn't difficult for people who speak German, so she made rapid progress. Now she hopes she will be able to make friends with more Americans. She also wants to get a driver's license. She has a German driver's license, but she needs to pass another test to be able to drive in the United States. She wants to pass it soon because she depends on a car to go everywhere.

Frank thinks he may be transferred overseas in a few months. Ursula is unhappy at the idea of moving again. When Frank was transferred to the United States, she was studying art at the university. Now she wants to stay in one place long enough to be able to finish her studies and begin working as an artist. She wants to stay in the United States or go back to Germany, but her husband thinks he may be sent to the Pacific.

B. Answer these questions.

1. Who is Ursula? 1. ____________________
2. When did they meet each other? 2. ____________________
3. What happened a year ago? 3. ____________________
4. Why did she make rapid progress in English? 4. ____________________ ____________________
5. What else does she want? 5. ____________________
6. Why can't she drive in the United States? 6. ____________________ ____________________
7. Why does she want to pass the test soon? 7. ____________________ ____________________
8. Why is Ursula unhappy? 8. ____________________

9. What was she studying? 9. ______________________

10. What does she want now? 10. ______________________

11. Where does she want to live? 11. ______________________

12. Where does Frank think he may be sent? 12. ______________________

____

C. Dialogue

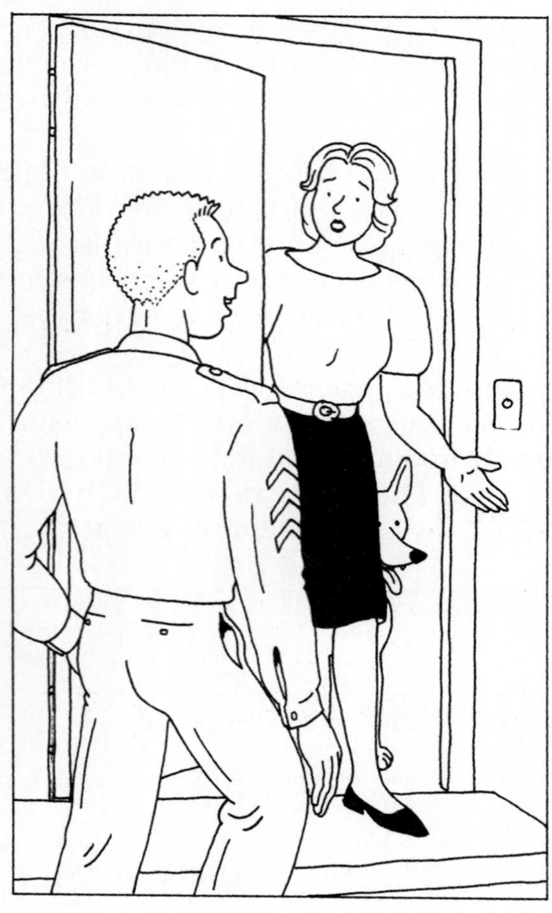

URSULA: You're late. Where have you been?
FRANK: I stopped at the base headquarters.
URSULA: Did you hear any news?
FRANK: Good news.
URSULA: Oh, Frank! What is it?
FRANK: We aren't going to be transferred.
URSULA: Are you sure?
FRANK: Yes, absolutely. We'll be stationed right here for two more years.
URSULA: Oh, wonderful! I've been so afraid of moving again.
FRANK: Well, not for two more years anyway.
URSULA: Now I can go back to school.
FRANK: First you have to take your driver's test.
URSULA: Do you think I'll pass? I'm worried about the written part of the test.
FRANK: You won't have any trouble with it.

Additional Vocabulary

advanced
army
art
artist
base (army base)
headquarters

license
(to) mail (out)
married
motel
(to) name
overseas

progress
rapid
responsible
sergeant
(to) station
study (n)

test
(to) transfer
unhappy
university
written

LESSON

15

FIFTEEN

REVIEW

Structure and Pattern Practice

A. Complete with the correct reflexive pronouns.

EXAMPLE

That boy talks about ___*himself*___ too much.

1. You people should laugh at ____________ more often.
2. She's going to the language lab to listen to ____________ on a tape recorder.
3. The students can listen to ____________ in the language lab.
4. I always look at ____________ in the mirror before I go out.
5. Did you hurt ____________ playing football?
6. We taught ____________ to do the exercises.

B. Combine these sentences, using *who* or *that* to connect them. The second sentence should become an adjective clause.

EXAMPLE

He's the student. He's going to give the speech.	*He's the student who's going to give the speech.*
1. Everybody liked the speech. He gave it at the ceremony.	1. ____________________
2. The young woman is going to graduate today. She's entering the gym now.	2. ____________________

3. The experiment can be dangerous. They're going to do it in the lab tomorrow. 3. ____________________

4. The student does careless work. He caused the accident. 4. ____________________

5. She always looks up the words. She doesn't understand them. 5. ____________________

C. Combine these sentences, using *that* to connect them. The second sentence should become an adjective clause.

EXAMPLE

I want to see the book. You're reading it now. *I want to see the book that you're reading now.*

1. That's the car. He just bought it. 1. ____________________

2. He's putting the things in the closet. He's not going to take them. 2. ____________________

3. I want to get ready for the exam. We're going to have it tomorrow. 3. ____________________

4. They like the word processor. They hired her last week. 4. ____________________

D. Change to the passive. Do not change the tense. Do not use a prepositional phrase to express the agent if the subject of the original sentence is a pronoun.

EXAMPLE

They sell women's clothes there. *Women's clothes are sold there.*

1. The teacher explained the lesson. 1. ____________________

2. Those men installed the new air conditioner. 2. ____________________

3. They transfer the employees every year. 3. ______________________________

4. His family owns this motel. 4. ______________________________

5. They put her in a math class. 5. ______________________________

6. They didn't allow him to enroll in an advanced class. 6. ______________________________

7. Did they require her to take a written test? 7. ______________________________

8. They don't mail out the students' grades. 8. ______________________________

E. Change to the passive. Follow the instructions for the previous exercise.

EXAMPLE

They've transferred the sergeant. *The sergeant has been transferred.*

1. The computer will improve work in the office. 1. ______________________________

2. Will they close the cafeteria during the summer? 2. ______________________________

3. They've sold all the merchandise. 3. ______________________________

4. His father had written the letter. 4. ______________________________

5. They should assign him to a new job. 5. ______________________________

6. Will they mail out the students' grades next week? 6. ______________________________

7. They haven't closed the office. 7. ______________________________

8. They can't transfer him overseas for two more years. 8. ______________________________

Reading and Conversation Practice

A. Read.

There aren't any students at the college during the last two weeks of August and the first two weeks of September. The summer classes end in the middle of August. The students for the fall semester don't arrive until the middle of September. However, there's a lot of activity on the campus during this time.

Workers clean all the buildings at the college while the students are away. Clerks and typists are at work in the administration building. They check the courses and grades of all the old students. They also check the high school records of the students who are going to enter the college in September. It is a busy time of year for the people who work for the college.

Many of the students will return to the college in the fall. Some of them are enjoying their vacations. Other students have found summer jobs to make a little money for the coming year. There were also many students who graduated in June. Most of them have already found jobs in the kind of work they studied for.

B. Answer these questions.

1. How many students are there at the college at the end of the summer? 1. ______________________________

____

____

2. When do the summer classes end? 2. ______________________________

3. When do the students for the fall semester arrive? 3. ______________________________

____

4. How much activity is there on the campus during this time? 4. ______________________________

____

5. What do workers do then? 5. ______________________________

6. Who is at work in the administration building? 6. ______________________________

____

7. What do the office workers check? 7. ______________________

____

8. What else do they check? 8. ______________________

9. Who is busy at this time of year? 9. ______________________

10. What will many of the students do? 10. ______________________

____

11. What are some of them doing? 11. ______________________

12. What have other students found? 12. ______________________

____

13. What happened to many students? 13. ______________________

____

14. What have most of these students found? 14. ______________________

____

C. Dialogue

CARL: What's our schedule today?
TONY: We're going to start cleaning the dormitories.
CARL: Are we going to do the men's or the women's first?
TONY: The men's. It's a bigger job.
CARL: Yes, there are always a lot of things that have to be fixed.
TONY: We'll only do one floor a day.
CARL: Well, that's not too bad.
TONY: But the whole building has to be finished this week.
CARL: That doesn't leave much time for the women's dorm.
TONY: It should be in better shape.
CARL: There's always too much work in the summer.
TONY: It's the only time of year when there aren't any students on the campus.
CARL: I'll be glad when they come back.
TONY: Oh, then they'll just start to make more work for us.